EXPERIENCING NIRVANA

NIRVANA

Grunge in Europe, 1989

A Microhistory by Bruce Pavitt

Edited by Dan Burke

B&W Photos by Steve Double

Bazillion Points

"Nirvana are Sub Pop's answer to the Beatles"

—Edwin Pouncey, *NME*, December 16, 1989

For Kurt. For Seattle.

EXPERIENCING NIRVANA
Grunge in Europe, 1989
A Microhistory by Bruce Pavitt

Second printing, published in 2014 by:

Bazillion Points
61 Greenpoint Ave. #504
Brooklyn, New York 11222
United States
www.bazillionpoints.com/nirvana
www.experiencingnirvana.com

Edited by Dan Burke
Produced for Bazillion Points by Ian Christe
Cover layout and design by Bazillion Points
Copyedited by Polly Watson

Foreword © Keith Cameron
Photographs © Bruce Pavitt except where noted
"Toiling at the Coalface of Pop Culture" essay and photographs © Steve Double
Additional photos by kind permission and © of the incredible Steve Double

A bazillion thank-yous to Nirvana, Mudhoney, Tad, Jon Poneman and Sub Pop Records,
Michael Pebworth, Steve Double, Keith Cameron, Andy Ryan, Magnus Henriksson,
Dianna Dilworth, Vivienne, James Lo, Erik Mans, Print Space NYC, Jeff Smith, Judy
Miller, Dick Busher, the Vera Project, and the good people of Italy, Switzerland, France,
Germany, Austria, the Netherlands, and England.

ISBN 978-1-935950-10-3

Printed in China

Interior title photo: *Kurt Cobain was the first person Jonathan Poneman and I encountered at the Piper Club, Rome, 11/27/89. Following pages: We ate dinner in a picturesque Italian restaurant prior to the Piper Club show. We just grabbed the first place we saw. Everything felt exotic and European—right down to the waiter's enormous mustache. This was a huge contrast to touring in the States. They served us salads with shaved fennel. We were ignorant American tourists—we had no idea what that flavor was. European fashion, design, and architecture operated at a level of sophistication far beyond our frame of reference. Imagine having lived—as Kurt and Krist had—in a small logging community like Aberdeen, WA, then being transported to some of the world's central cities. We were a little out of our league. The photos in this book represent to me the wonderment and sudden personal growth that can happen when you step into a much richer environment. First dinner overleaf: Bassist Krist Novoselic of Nirvana and Sub Pop Records co-founder Jonathan Poneman. Second dinner overleaf: Kurt Cobain and drummer Chad Channing of Nirvana. Dedication photo: Nirvana, LameFest UK, 12/3/89*

CONTENTS

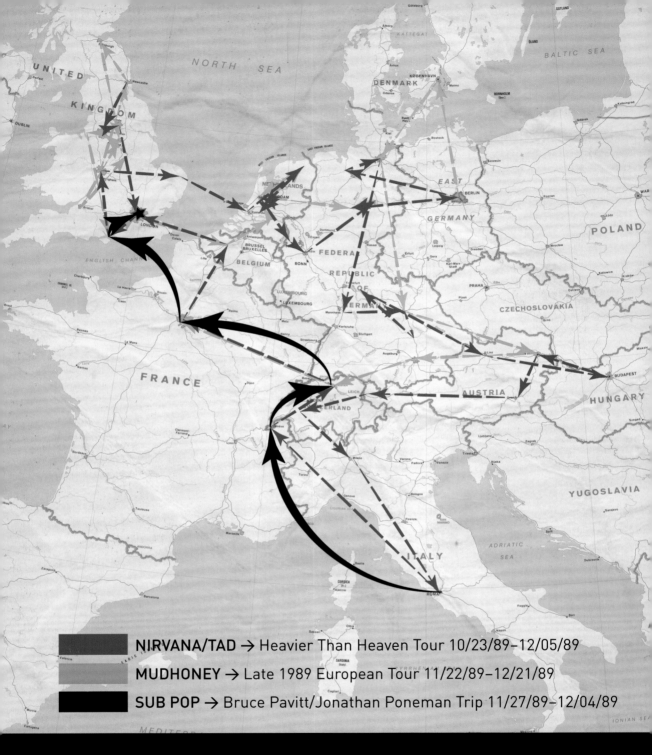

NIRVANA/TAD → Heavier Than Heaven Tour 10/23/89–12/05/89
MUDHONEY → Late 1989 European Tour 11/22/89–12/21/89
SUB POP → Bruce Pavitt/Jonathan Poneman Trip 11/27/89–12/04/89

NIRVANA

Kurt Cobain—vocals and guitar
Krist Novoselic—bass guitar
Chad Channing—drums

TAD

Tad Doyle—vocals and guitar
Gary Thorstensen—guitar
Kurt Danielson—bass guitar
Steve Wied—drums

MUDHONEY

Mark Arm—vocals and guitar
Steve Turner—guitar
Matt Lukin—bass guitar
Dan Peters—drums

SUB POP

Bruce Pavitt, Executive Chairman of Supervisory Management
Jonathan Poneman, Supervisory Chairman of Executive Management

Grunge in Europe, 1989
Tour Dates

NIRVANA / TAD, Heavier Than Heaven tour:

10/23/89 Riverside, Newcastle Upon Tyne, UK
10/24/89 Students' Union, Polytechnic, Manchester, UK
10/25/89 Duchess of York, Leeds, UK
10/27/89 Student Union, The School of Oriental and African
　　　　 Studies, London
10/28/89 Ents Hall, Polytechnic, Portsmouth, UK
10/29/89 Edwards No. 8, Birmingham, UK
10/30/89 The Wilde Club, Norwich Arts Centre, Norwich, UK
11/01/89 Nighttown, Rotterdam, The Netherlands
11/02/89 Vera, Groningen, The Netherlands
11/03/89 Tivoli, Utrecht, The Netherlands
11/04/89 Gigant, Apeldoorn, The Netherlands
11/05/89 Melkweg, Amsterdam
11/07/89 B/52, Moenchengladbach, West Germany
11/08/89 Rose Club, Cologne, West Germany
11/09/89 Bad, Hanover, West Germany
11/10/89 Forum Enger, Enger, West Germany
11/11/89 Ecstasy, West Berlin
11/12/89 Kulturzentrum, Oldenburg, West Germany
11/13/89 The Fabrik, Hamburg, West Germany
11/15/89 Schwimmbad Musik-Club, Heidelberg, West
　　　　 Germany
11/16/89 Trust, Nuremberg, West Germany
11/17/89 Circus, Gammelsdorf, West Germany
11/18/89 Kultur-Basar, Hanau, West Germany
11/20/89 Kapu, Linz, Austria
11/21/89 Petõfi Csarnok, Budapest, Hungary
11/22/89 U4, Vienna
11/23/89 Cafe Pi, Graz, Austria
11/24/89 Konkret, Hohenems, Austria
11/25/89 Fri-Son, Fribourg, Switzerland
11/26/89 Bloom, Mezzago, Italy
11/27/89 Piper Club, Rome
11/29/89 l'Usine, Geneva
11/30/89 Rote Fabrik, Zürich
12/01/89 Le Fahrenheit, Issy-les-Moulineaux, France
12/02/89 Democrazy, Ghent, Belgium
12/03/89 LameFest UK, Astoria Theatre, London
12/05/89 Maida Vale 5, John Peel Session, London

MUDHONEY late 1989 European tour:

11/22/89 Edwards No. 8, Birmingham, UK
11/23/89 Riverside, Newcastle, UK
11/25/89 Calton Road Studios, Edinburgh, Scotland
11/26/89 University, Sheffield, UK
11/27/89 Bierkeller, Bristol, UK
11/29/89 Trent Polytechnic, Nottingham, UK
11/30/89 Polytechnic, Liverpool, UK
12/01/89 International I, Manchester, UK
12/02/89 Polytechnic, Portsmouth, UK
12/03/89 LameFest UK, Astoria Theatre, London
12/04/89 Astoria Theatre, London
12/05/89 Demo Crazy, Ghent, Belgium
12/07/89 Willem II, Den Bosh, The Netherlands
12/08/89 Tivoli, Utrecht, The Netherlands
12/09/89 Vera, Groningen, The Netherlands
12/10/89 Melkweg, Amsterdam
12/11/89 Cafe Europa, Bielefeld, West Germany
12/12/89 The Loft, Berlin
12/14/89 Barbue, Copenhagen
12/15/89 Fabrik, Hamburg, West Germany
12/16/89 Rührersaal, Nuremberg, West Germany
12/17/89 U4, Vienna
12/18/89 *Mudhoney joined Soul Asylum onstage during the
encore of a Soul Asylum show in Munich*
12/19/89 Theaterfabrik, Munich
12/20/89 Rote Fabrik, Zürich
12/21/89 Cirque Anne Frateline, Paris

Overleaf: *Mark Arm of Mudhoney bends over backwards for rock and roll. Kurt Cobain is the onstage spectator wearing scarf and holding aluminum beer can, LameFest UK, 12/3/89* PHOTO BY STEVE DOUBLE.

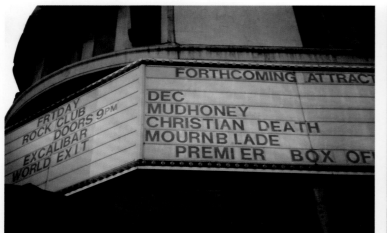

LameFest UK: Our Turn, at Last

Keith Cameron

LameFest UK was both the culmination of a process and the beginning of a new revolutionary era that would ultimately change the sound of late-twentieth-century rock music. All the bands that played London's Astoria Theatre on the evening of Sunday, December 3, 1989, had played the city earlier that year. Tad and Nirvana had appeared on October 27, as part of their co-headlining debut UK tour. In fact, Mudhoney was now making its third UK visit in a calendar year. During that time, Seattle's Sub Pop record label had established itself as an identifiable signifier of a specific strand of rock music. The label issued a series of brilliant records backed up by the enthusiastic validation of key media outlets; notably, John Peel's BBC Radio program and the weekly music press.

Though these three bands were individually distinct in regard to the specifics of their sounds and temperaments, having them play together helped foster a collective identity. Sub Pop correctly believed this grouping would appeal to audience members' natural desire to feel like participants in a social movement, rather than mere spectators at an exhibition—as is typical of the routine mainstream rock experience.

One phenomenon of LameFest UK was a massive queue for the merchandise stall. Upon arriving at the venue shortly after 7:30 P.M., I noticed that the line was already extending up the stairs, beyond the entrance, to the hall itself. Nirvana, the night's opening band, began its set to a relatively thin crowd, because so many people wanted to buy T-shirts. In addition to commemorative LameFest UK garments, each band had its own shirts for sale. Among these were two soon-to-be-legendary designs: Mudhoney's Big Muff pedal artwork, and Nirvana's FUDGE PACKIN, CRACK SMOKIN, SATAN WORSHIPIN, MOTHERFUCKERS shirt. Everything was branded with the Sub Pop logo on the back.

Many who chose to wait in line for Nirvana shirts that evening would not have actually been able to see the band play. Those who decided to watch Nirvana were rewarded with a staggering performance, one that duly consoled them upon their return to the merch stall to

Facing page, from top: *LameFest UK happened here at the Astoria Theatre, London. The headliner, Mudhoney, was listed on the marquee, while the lesser-known Nirvana and Tad were not mentioned; Once the music began, the crowd went wild. Note fearless* Sounds *photographer Steve Double front of stage, shooting photos.*

discover that all the Nirvana T-shirts had been sold. Thus, in their desire to be visibly acknowledged as part of a community as well as via their hysteric dance rituals, the audience became actors in a "happening"—something bigger than a mere rock gig.

The seismic cultural shift that occurred with Nirvana's *Nevermind* album was the ultimate consequence of an unstoppable momentum, built upon the perception of a common cause, established to no small degree at LameFest UK. The bands were not just representing themselves: They were also "Seattle bands" and "Sub Pop bands"—cogs in a bigger wheel, which they were pivotal in turning. In the twelve months following December 3, 1989, the media profile of all three bands grew, thanks to the swift transmission of information enabled by the mutually combative ethos of the weekly UK music magazines and the country's geographical compactness. Sub Pop well knew that stuff happened in Britain much quicker than in the US.

Nirvana's next UK tour, in October 1990, saw them sell out clubs and theaters across the country, without even a new record to promote. That same summer, Mudhoney enjoyed a three-night residency in London and went on to star at the Reading Festival in front of a crowd of thirty-five thousand. Meanwhile, Tad's gregarious and funny front man became something of a figurehead, a Sub Pop star.

In a broader context, many of the UK groups, including Senseless Things and Mega City Four, that had opened up for their Sub Pop brethren also landed major record deals. And audiences at rock shows began loosening up and exhibiting more liberated attitudes, comparable to those found amid the burgeoning rave culture. None of this could have happened without the bands themselves doing the thing that they did: playing rock 'n' roll with a transformative purpose and abandon that virtually no one amid the UK's buttoned-up, battened-down populace had ever before witnessed.

The colossal misconception regarding subsequent events is that music from this time and place was downcast or depressing. The music that became known as grunge—as showcased in its purest form in London on December 3, 1989—was a fount of joy. For sure, there was turbulence within the sound, serving as a conduit for inner strife, but on the most basic level the music was sheer fun. I was lucky enough to meet all three LameFest bands that night in the beery fug of the Astoria's main dressing room, where smiles and good cheer were the only currency available. The people leaving the hall downstairs looked and felt exactly the same.

Outsiders together, this was our time.

Our turn.

At last.

Nirvana, LameFest, 12/3/89

Nirvana...Was Experienced

Bruce Pavitt

We didn't have much to work with.

When Jon Poneman and I quit our day jobs and opened the doors to the official Sub Pop Records office on April 1, 1988, we didn't have any bands with us. Soundgarden had already departed the label, and Green River had just broken up. In short, although we knew Seattle was developing a distinctive brand of heavy, soulful, grungy rock, we weren't sure who our next bands were going to be. Then everything unfolded.

On April 10, a Sunday night a short time after, a young trio named Nirvana played a showcase for Jon and me at the Central Tavern in Pioneer Square. Aside from the band, four people were in the club: Jon, the doorman, the bartender, and me. Although the large room was empty, the band showed promise. We signed them up for a seven-inch single, "Love Buzz," their cover of a 1969 Shocking Blue song. Nirvana didn't have much stage presence or a lot of material, but singer Kurt Cobain had a great voice. We both agreed that Nirvana had potential. They must have thought the same of us. After a while, they eventually signed to Sub Pop for six hundred dollars—which we couldn't even afford to pay them—plus a written commitment on our part to come up with more cash for their next record.

A few days later, on Friday, April 15, a new band named Mudhoney entered Reciprocal Recording in Seattle with ace producer Jack Endino and recorded two songs: "Touch Me I'm Sick" and "Sweet Young Thing (Ain't Sweet No More)." Mark Arm—the front man of Green River—had formed this new group, which sounded like a fuzzed-out version of the Sonics crossed with the Stooges. On Tuesday, April 19, at the Vogue nightclub in Belltown, Mudhoney played its first show, on a bill with Seattle's up-and-coming Blood Circus and New York's Das Damen. The show was well-attended, and the music was raw, powerful, and seriously awesome. This incredible out-of-the-box performance gave us the hope and inspiration we needed. The sound of our record label was coming into focus.

Facing page: I had a very utilitarian tourist uniform, and I literally wore the same clothes from Rome to England. Every day I put on my sweatshirt from Harvey Mudd College that cost me a dollar at a thrift store, and I'd throw on my Carhartt jacket and my huntsman cap. A lot of the Seattle scene was very enamored with cheap, simple, timeless, work clothes, this Carhartt jacket being a perfect example. With my new wave and punk background, I wanted to give Northwest lumberjack culture a deeper twist, so I commissioned a friend of mine to add the bear artwork, which emphasized the Northwest mystique. People could instantly tell I was from the United States. That was my uniform, just like the Ramones had uniforms. I did change my underwear.

Meanwhile, Tad Doyle, a heavyset musical prodigy from Boise, had recorded an angular, raging two-song demo over at Reciprocal, featuring the songs "Ritual Device" and "Daisy." An ex-butcher who previously played jazz drums, Tad had worked alongside Mark Arm and me at the Muzak corporation. On his demo, not only did Tad provide vocals, but he managed impressively to play everything: guitar, bass, and drums. Jon and I decided to release this brilliant recording as another single on Sub Pop. Tad Doyle soon grouped with other musicians to form a touring and recording band, simply called Tad, and that band eventually released three full-length records on our label.

Fast-forward to December 3, 1989.

Jon and I were convinced that the way to break the "Seattle sound" to the U.S. and the rest of the globe was to win the support of the British music press, the most influential music media at the time. Although our bands were sub-popular and ignored by the mainstream American press, they soon endeared themselves to some very influential tastemakers in the UK, including BBC Radio DJ John Peel and music critic Everett ("The Legend") True of *Melody Maker*. We hoped that by bringing three of our best acts—Nirvana, Tad, and Mudhoney—directly to London for a well-hyped showcase, we could establish Sub Pop and Seattle grunge as international phenomenons.

To this end, we created LameFest UK, held on December 3, 1989, at the two-thousand-capacity Astoria Theatre in London. This showcase was modeled after the infamous, sold-out Seattle LameFest, which had taken place six months prior, on June 9, at the Moore Theatre in our hometown, and had been an unbridled success. In both cases, Sub Pop took three of the greatest undiscovered rock bands in history and put them in front of a sizable audience. The Seattle response was historic. Could we reasonably expect the same ecstatic response from a jaded, seen-it-all London crowd? As it so happened, yes we could.

From Kurt Cobain's first broken string, the crowd reaction was relentless, with constant stage diving and crowd surfing. Amps were turned up loud, and guitars were smashed. Although headliners Mudhoney were in top form, opening act Nirvana caught everybody by surprise. That night in London, Nirvana revealed its power and presence, along with the guttural voice of Kurt Cobain, a sound that would come to affect a generation. This performance officially marked the beginning of Nirvana's ascension. Within two years, the band would rocket up the global pop charts with *Nevermind*, the first punk-influenced record to reach number one in the United States and many other countries. Britain, with its influential scene, was now put on notice. From here on out, grunge and Nirvana would only grow bigger.

Nirvana, Tad, and Mudhoney—a crew of fellow "losers" hustling outside of a rigged corporate system—had ultimately established a new set of values and ushered in a new era of populist rock. On their watch, music was all about heart and soul, even if it meant missing notes and chords and losing one's balance. Shows were about getting loose and letting go. There was no barrier between bands and fans. It was one big party.

Anyone who attended these intimate, early performances knows what the energy felt like: amazing. Time slowed down. Gravity was defied. Miracles were witnessed, and blessings were received. Ecstasy was induced, and Nirvana...was experienced.

I had been to Europe for two weeks in the spring of '87, after earning some money from the sale of the first Sub Pop record, Sub Pop 100. I went to Amsterdam and, of course, immediately went to my first hash bar. I also traveled to Belgium and the UK. At some point, I remember seeing a huge poster of Sylvester Stallone as Rocky. I had a profound epiphany about how much Europe loved America, and what a powerful export American culture was. After that, there was no doubt in my mind that Sub Pop could find a market for American music around the rest of the world. Until I actually went to another country and saw how American culture was worshipped, I didn't fully get it. That insight became a huge incentive for me to focus the label on Seattle. Jonathan Poneman was not overly familiar with Europe, but he had a great interest in traveling. We both wanted to see the records we were putting out be appreciated globally. We both thought the music we loved could become a phenomenon. In other words, we were both delusional—but it seemed to work out.

DAY 1
Piper Club → Rome
Monday, November 27

Jon and I arrived in Rome to connect with two of the new Seattle groups we were working with: Nirvana and Tad. Our mission was to assist in any way possible prior to their big Sub Pop showcase in London (LameFest UK), where they were to perform with their headlining labelmates Mudhoney. The British media was notorious for launching music careers, and we hoped that this event would be a defining moment for the artists.

In particular, we were concerned about Kurt Cobain, singer for Nirvana, as we had heard that he was feeling resigned and homesick, and was suffering from exhaustion. Jon and I were hoping to help raise his spirits with a show of support. Everyone knew that it was crucial for the bands to arrive in London in good shape, as the three-band LameFest UK was by far the biggest show of the tour, with the potential to have a huge impact via the influential British press.

That afternoon, after taking some time to explore St. Peter's Square, we met up with Nirvana and Tad at the legendary Piper Club, where the bands were finishing up their soundchecks. After almost five weeks on the road, the artists were tired but glad to see us. We went out for some pasta and then headed back to the venue as fans started to show up.

The Tad band got onstage and started their aggressive, lumbering set, showcasing tracks from their debut album, *God's Balls*. Taunting the crowd, bass player Kurt Danielson fell into the audience, yelling, "Fuck the Pope!" while drummer Steve Wied kept the beat. After forty minutes of provoking the Rome citizenry, the world's heaviest band then retired upstairs to recuperate.

Nirvana's turn was next. Kurt approached the mic, made a few comments, and then started screaming, testing the limits of the microphone. As the crowd rushed towards the stage, Nirvana broke into "School." The song had a great hook, and the band often used it to open their shows.

Facing page: *Nirvana, Piper Club, Rome, 11/27/89*

Above: Jon Poneman and I were very very different, and therefore ridiculously complementary. Once we came into a meeting, and somebody commented: "Here comes the left brain and the right brain." Jon was brilliantly logical. I would rather live in the realm of imagination, making things up as I went along. Jon was a vegetarian and a meditator, and I was a partying omnivore. We had different lifestyles and different ways of thinking, and that's what made Sub Pop interesting.

"School" featured a repetitive, trance-inducing lyrical style that the band would eventually make famous. "I'm in high school again," Kurt mumbled, bringing down the energy, before kicking back into a loud roar: "No recess!" Kurt and bass player Krist Novoselic were loose, moving across the entire stage. Despite their exhaustion, the band found some energy.

Their frenetic performance, clearly influenced by Mudhoney, had come a long way since the first time I saw them in Seattle—they were much more animated and intense. The band played more songs from *Bleach*: "Scoff," "Floyd the Barber," and their Beatlesque pop tune "About a Girl." They roared into "Love Buzz" and "Big Cheese" from their first Sub Pop single. A few newer tunes were in the mix as well: "Polly," "Imodium" (later released as "Breed"), and "Been a Son," as well as an ultra-heavy track called "Dive." With more than thirty European shows now behind them, the band looked and sounded ferocious.

Then it happened.

Ten songs into their set, Kurt, frustrated with his guitar, smashed it completely and climbed a tall stack of speakers. The crowd looked on, with many drunk spectators yelling, "Jump!" It was a dramatic moment, potentially harmful. I witnessed the event from the club floor, stunned, while Jon and Tad looked down from the artists area on the second floor. Everyone was holding their breath, not sure if Kurt would actually jump. We were panicked, and extremely concerned for Kurt's well-being.

Several minutes went by while Kurt kept threatening to jump. Finally, after much cajoling from the security staff, he climbed back down to safety. He was then immediately confronted by the sound tech, who claimed that Kurt had trashed the club's vocal mic. As is now legend, Kurt grabbed the microphone and exclaimed, "Damaged? Now it's damaged!" while throwing it on the floor.

Kurt, distressed, hung out backstage and spent some time talking to his friend Tad, processing the night's events. A while later, after checking in with Krist and drummer Chad Channing, the band decided the stress was too much and decided to break up. Kurt had reached his limit.

After some time, Jon, who had a close relationship with Kurt, went outside and walked around the block for a heart-to-heart with his friend. While the rest of the musicians loaded up the van, Kurt confided that he had looked out into the crowd that night and seen, "the kind of guys who used to beat me up in high school."

Playing to friends in Olympia and Seattle was a different experience, marked by camaraderie and crowd surfing; being on the road was more challenging, as the band oftentimes performed for crowds that were more "metal" (or macho). Despite the muscular power of Nirvana's punk-pop, Kurt was essentially a sensitive guy who did not feel comfortable in high-testosterone social environments. That night he questioned everything, and simply wanted to go back home and be with his girlfriend.

Hoping to keep the band together, Jon offered a train ticket to Geneva to Kurt, so that he could arrive at the next show refreshed. By taking the train instead of packing into the van, Kurt could take a day off in Rome, go sightseeing with us, and relax before playing the next show in Switzerland on Wednesday night. Jon also offered to buy Kurt a new guitar. After these overtures, Kurt chilled out, and he decided to continue on with Nirvana.

This page, top: *Girls in black hose passing by Mr. Muscle in favor of some American rock bands.* This page, bottom: *Our Italian distributor and support team were very happy with the positive reviews the tour had received.* Facing page, top: *Check out Tad bassist Kurt Danielson's sweater. Artful thrifting was a huge part of grunge culture. In order to live on the cheap, we had to creatively navigate thrift stores. The coolest thing you could find would be some incredibly crazy trucker hat or a sweater like that; that would be your statement, at a kingly cost of fifty-nine cents. Grunge fashion, if you want to call it that, began as an ironic appropriation of logger redneck culture, and that was a shared, instinctively agreed-upon part of all our lives.* Facing page, bottom: *Jon Poneman with Tad guitarist Gary Thorstensen*

Above: *Tad opened for Nirvana that night and totally raged; Bass player Kurt Danielson falls onto the crowd; Italian fans in leather jackets and turtlenecks; Yellow flannel in Rome. Seattle still had a working-class feel in 1989. Now it's a completely different city. The food and coffee culture was just starting to bloom in 1989. Today Seattle is truly a cosmopolitan city, several notches* up. *Everything has shifted to the reality of Amazon and Microsoft versus Boeing and Weyerhauser. The whole flannel-shirted, parka vibe that felt so natural to us in 1989 just has no place there any more. If you walk around today wearing flannel and work boots—which I actually do—you're seen as kind of a freak. Facing page: The Tad band.*

Facing page: *Tad live*. Above: *The Piper Club. Note the TV wall* Overleaf: *Tad Doyle and Jonathan Poneman*

Above: *Jon Poneman and Tad Doyle watch Nirvana from the rafters.*

Facing page: *Nirvana's set took a tumultuous turn. During "Spank Thru," Kurt smashed his only guitar, then climbed a tall stack of speakers and began motioning that he planned to jump. Fortunately, the security staff talked him down, but he destroyed a club microphone. Very distraught, Kurt announced to Jon* *that Nirvana was breaking up. This page, from top: After the show, Jon walked around the block with Kurt to calm him down, while the others loaded the van; Tad and I waited for word from our friends. Overleaf: Kurt and Jon in conference. By morning, Nirvana had decided to stay together.*

It felt good to see Kurt open up. Although generally quiet, he would come alive when discussing music. The Pixies, Beat Happening, the Vaselines, Black Flag. We really connected that day as indie-music geeks.

After some conversation, we realized that the first time we were in a room together was at a Black Flag show—Tuesday, September 25, 1984, at the Mountaineers Club in Seattle. We noted that Mudhoney's Mark Arm and Steve Turner were in the room that night as well, performing with Green River. Kurt had gone to the show with his roommate Matt Lukin (who would later join Mudhoney) and Buzz Osborne, both of Aberdeen's Melvins. We agreed it was an amazing show, and that the heavy tempo of Black Flag's new sound had challenged the punk culture. The dots had yet to connect, but it seemed the grunge scene had started with that show.

I shared an anecdote with Kurt; I told him that I had interviewed Black Flag's Henry Rollins and guitarist Greg Ginn on my KCMU Sub Pop radio hour that night, in between playing tracks from the band's *My War* album. I'd asked Henry, the singer: "Is Black Flag going heavy metal?" He responded, "Heavy mental!" Kurt thought that was amusing.

I reflected back on my first encounter with Kurt. Although we had attended some of the same shows, I hadn't met him until the fall of 1987 in Olympia, when Candice Pedersen of K Records had introduced us. He and his girlfriend Tracy Marander were friendly and had invited me into their Pear Street apartment. I remembered that she wore a Melvins T-shirt, and that he wore flannel. Entering their space, I noticed they had some rock posters pinned to the wall, including one of Queen. They had many small pets in cages, including an aggressive rat, which unfortunately bit my finger. Kurt did not mention he was in a band, though he had proudly told me he was a roadie for the Melvins. My first impression was that Kurt was shy, sincere, and creative. I noticed that Tracy did most of the talking.

As I came back into the moment, I continued walking through the streets of Rome, enjoying the sun and the conversations as the day progressed. Having already viewed the Coliseum, we decided to head over to the Vatican to view Saint Peter's Basilica and the Sistine Chapel.

Entering Saint Peter's was a profound experience. Built during the Renaissance, it's one of the largest Christian churches in the world, and its ornate interior is beyond description.

Every one of us was silent. This was a far cry from the Piper Club.

We checked out the Apostolic Palace, the official residence of the Pope. Once inside,

Facing page: Kurt was noticeably affected by the night before and took some time alone to think. Originally, Jon and I were just going to London, specifically to network, meet with our publicist, visit Rough Trade, and talk to Reinhardt Holstein, our European representative.

Then we heard that Kurt in particular was having a very hard time on the Heavier Than Heaven tour, so we wound up going to Rome. We had heard that he was losing it, and the rumors were correct. I'm glad we showed up. The Rome detour was a last-minute thing.

we strolled through the Sistine Chapel, and witnessed the genius of Michelangelo's biblical narratives painted on the ceiling. We viewed the nine scenes outlining the Christian story of creation and the downfall of humanity. Feeling somewhat overwhelmed, we exited through the gift shop, stopping briefly to check out some souvenir cherubs. It had been a long day with a lot of walking. We stopped at a trattoria and drank some cappuccinos. We noted how finely dressed the people of Rome were. The culture there was very refined. I was humbled by the beauty of the people and of the city.

At the train station, we discussed the tour. Both Kurt and Steve, who were still pretty worn down, were feeling they could reasonably hit their stride and finish the last few dates—a few shows in Switzerland, one in France, one in Belgium, and then the big one with Mudhoney in London—before returning to Seattle. All we had to do next was get on the train and sleep through the night until we arrived in Geneva.

Facing page: *I'm sure there was some sticker shock involved with buying a new guitar in Rome, but the gift of the guitar to Kurt was a sincere gesture of support for a friend who was having a hard time. He had just trashed his last guitar and announced that his band was breaking up. He did not want to continue to the epic London showcase that would eventually launch him as an international star. I do remember that our funds were tight, but we needed to make a sincere offer of cooperation. That's how mom-and-pop indie businesses operate; it's essentially an extended family—or a tribe. You do what you can to help your friends out. I think the guitar lasted another week, but so be it.*

Above: *Tad and NIrvana and crew prepare to head to Switzerland, loading up the van driven by tour manager Edwin Heath. This Fiat van ultimately hauled seven musicians, one soundman, one tour manager, and all the gear across Europe through the whole Heavier*

Than Heaven tour: Thirty-six shows in forty-two days in nine countries. Jon Poneman, Kurt Cobain, Steve Wied, and I parted ways with the others here, as we remained in Rome for the day before taking a late train to Switzerland.

I grew up in an agnostic household, never going to church, and I was essentially raised to believe that the Bible was a collection of fairy stories. This trip still had a spiritual dimension for me, in that the beauty and refined aesthetics of Rome were truly awe-inspiring. I believe that spirituality has a lot to do with getting in touch with that sense of awe. Overleaf: Kurt browsing the gift shop at St. Peter's Basilica. Jon and I are visible in the mirror reflection.

DAY 3
L'Usine → Geneva
Wednesday, November 29

We woke up the next morning at the Swiss border, and there was a problem. The previous night, before going to sleep, Kurt had placed his passport and his wallet in his shoes. Later, someone had quietly opened the door and made off with both his wallet and passport. Traveling as a group, we could not enter Switzerland until a temporary visa for Kurt was issued.

Jon and I stepped in and helped Kurt navigate the Swiss bureaucracy. With paperwork complete, we got back on the train and headed toward Geneva, where the tour van would be waiting to pick us up. I realized that within the past twenty-four hours we had assisted Kurt in acquiring a new guitar and a temporary visa. We had also helped to provide a day of downtime so that Kurt could recuperate and experience the cultural wonders of Rome. We knew that touring was hard work, and it felt good to provide some support.

Arriving in Geneva, Kurt was eager to call home and talk to his girlfriend. After a quick breakfast, Kurt and Jon made their way to a telephone booth. Jon offered the use of an international calling card that we used for label business. After Kurt connected with Tracy, the tour van pulled up. We got in and made our way to our hotel. Things seemed like they were back on track.

That night at Club L'Usine, Nirvana busted out Leadbelly's "Where Did You Sleep Last Night" for the first time. I noted that Nirvana had a strong history of sharing songs by other artists. It was this type of sharing that helped keep indie-rock culture vital.

While the six-week Tad/Nirvana European tour was almost complete, Mudhoney had only recently started theirs. That night Mudhoney was playing its sixth show, tearing it up in Nottingham, UK. Jon and I would be meeting up with them in Portsmouth in three days, with everyone finally convening on December 3 at LameFest UK. All sights were now on London

Facing page: Jon Poneman lays down 10,000 lira for three cappuccinos prior to our departure.

and the two-thousand-capacity Astoria Theatre. It would be, by far, the biggest venue Nirvana had ever played.

I knew in my heart that grunge was going to blow up. Although the genre had its roots in the punk scene, it was more populist. The singing was soulful and the recordings had warmth. The songwriting was good and occasionally brilliant. Also, with the Sub Pop bands in particular, there was humor and a sense of irreverence. Above all, however, the live shows were manic, ecstatic, and liberating. No matter where they went, the response to Nirvana, Tad, and Mudhoney was almost always, "Oh my God."

I thought about some of the current trends in music. The indie scene in America had a diverse mix of highly respected groups, such as Fugazi from DC, Beat Happening from Olympia, and Sonic Youth from NYC. Although all of these bands were brilliant and idealistic, I felt they were too idiosyncratic to cross over to a larger audience. The bands we worked with were less stylized and less conceptual, typically triggering a more immediate physical response, and from a wider group of fans.

In addition to the maturity of indie culture in the U.S., other trends were happening. In the corporate world, LA glam was still the dominant commercial force in American rock. Guns N' Roses, Poison, Faster Pussycat, and Mötley Crüe were huge, although the superficiality of these bands was considered suspect by most fans going to indie/grunge shows in Seattle. Jane's Addiction, however, was a creative LA club band that crossed over and appealed to glam rockers as well as the indie scene. I remember seeing a copy of the band's debut studio album, *Nothing's Shocking*, in Krist Novoselic's personal record collection. Soundgarden also opened for them at Seattle's Paramount Theater in November of 1988.

Hip hop was reaching a critical apex during the late '80s. Four albums in particular stood out from this time: Public Enemy's *It Takes a Nation of Millions to Hold Us Back*, Eric B. and Rakim's *Follow the Leader*, NWA's *Straight Outta Compton*, and the Beastie Boys' *Paul's Boutique*. These artists got a lot of play at after-hours parties in Seattle. The first time I heard *Straight Outta Compton*, I was in San Francisco driving around with Nirvana.

In the UK, the "Madchester" scene of danceable, psychedelic indie rock was blowing up, but not in Seattle. Although the Stone Roses and Happy Mondays dominated the covers of the UK weeklies while we were in England, there seemed to be little enthusiasm for the genre back home in the Pacific Northwest. However, Manchester bands who gained UK popularity in the early '80s, like New Order and the Smiths, received a lot of airplay on the local indie radio station, KCMU, for many years.

Although many divergent musical styles were in play in late 1989, I believed that Seattle grunge was poised to break out of the underground and into the mainstream in a way that would surprise everybody.

We left Rome Termini Station after dark and slept on the overnight train to Geneva.

When we arrived at the Geneva train station that morning, Kurt woke up and realized his passport and wallet had been stolen. Here Jonathan is helping Kurt make a calling card call to his girlfriend in Olympia, WA, to tell her what had happened. Kurt had placed his passport and wallet in his shoes, which were near the sliding glass door of his compartment. In the night, someone had slid open the door and taken the wallet and the passport. That was a huge upset for everybody. The whole point of the train trip was to give Kurt and Steve Wied from the Tad band some time to recuperate from nervous exhaustion.

We headed straight to our hotel after the tour van met us at the Geneva train station. Instead of relaxing, we had a stressful situation and a major bit of drama. I tried to keep my cool, but the mood was heavy.

DAY 4
Rote Fabrik → Zürich
Thursday, November 30

Around noon, Jon and I boarded a train and headed northwest to Zürich, Switzerland, while the musicians continued traveling by van, stopping over at the American Embassy in Bern to secure an official passport for Kurt.

We both looked forward to another raucous Tad/Nirvana show, which that night was to be held at the infamous Rote Fabrik cultural center, located on the edge of Lake Zürich in a converted electronics factory.

Arriving at the city center late that afternoon, we took a bus down to Rote Fabrik. As we looked out the window, we realized how wealthy the city was. Zürich was the banking center of Europe, and its downtown appeared clean and orderly.

When we arrived at the venue, located a few miles south of the city center, in Old Town, we took note of the graffiti that seemed to cover much of the entrance. The red, brick building had seen some use, and provided a contrast to the conservative downtown area we had just traveled through. Posters promoting the night's show, featuring a picture of the Tad band, were prominent in the entrance. Nirvana was only mentioned in small type, and was obviously considered an opening act.

With time on our hands, we went for a walk near the lake, taking in a view of alpine silhouettes in the distance. The scene was beautiful and reminded me of Seattle. As we headed back to the club, we noticed a poster for an upcoming Mudhoney show on a telephone pole. Seattle grunge was working its way through Europe, and we were stoked.

That night at the show, the Tad band cranked up the volume and burned through most of their *God's Balls* album, plus a newer track called "Wood Goblins." The crowd was a bit older and seemed to connect with Tad's more complex arrangements. They delivered a crushing performance.

Nirvana had stepped out and missed most of the Tad show. They arrived at the venue just in time to get it together. Kurt's new songs, like "Been a Son" and "Imodium," were simple and dynamic, and sounded great. By now, I had to admit that Nirvana's songwriting and kinetic live show were both beginning to rival those of their superstar brethren Mudhoney, who were raging away in Liverpool at that moment.

At the end of the night, we were all invited to an after-hours party held within another part of the three-story arts center. Rote Fabrik was unlike anything in the U.S. The center housed a government-subsidized collective with more than sixty live-in artist studios, bringing together a community of musicians, painters, filmmakers, and designers. The gathering we attended was in a large, noncommercial common area; the DJ music was very eclectic and varied from punk to free jazz to world music. Rote Fabrik was inspiring, and we left thinking that Europe had a lot to teach America.

Previous: *Rote Fabrik, a former factory building located in Zürich's Old Town, was extremely unusual. The entire compound was a state-sponsored art collective—truly socialism in action. The facility included many different art spaces, plus a public commons where shows took place. I had never seen anything like it. You can see in the crowd shots that a lot of these people were older. I got the feeling that they were art students, or artists. Zürich was not a teen hardcore crowd at all. I came away feeling very impressed by Rote Fabrik and the people who supported us there. The Vera Project in Seattle would be possibly a counterpart, an art and music center sponsored by the city that is a great asset to contemporary Seattle.*

The amount of graffiti inside Rote Fabrik blew us away. Jon grabbed a poster off the wall for that night's show to keep as a souvenir. The after-hours party was probably the most interesting night of the tour. We went to a loft space in the compound, and the party host was spinning a wild variety of music. Coming from an American club and party culture, I was just humbled by the intelligence of what I experienced. Overleaf: The Tad band live were tremendous. Following pages: After great performances the backstage atmosphere was upbeat, which was good news, as LameFest UK was now only three days away.

MEN DRESS AS LADIES
WHEN I DIE I HOPE THEY BURY ME UPSIDE DOWN SO THEN THE WHOLE WORLD CAN KISS MY ASS
90°
I LOVE MONEY
ERIC IDLE

DAY 5
Lost in Reflections → Paris
Friday, December 1

After a late night in Zürich, Jon and I woke up, said goodbye to the crew, and boarded yet another train, this one headed northwest to Paris. Our plan was to visit the city, then connect with Mudhoney the following night in Portsmouth, UK.

As was typical whenever we were together, Jon and I brainstormed, and the lengthy ride gave us plenty of time to talk. Our record company, Sub Pop, presented an endless series of challenges and opportunities, so we were always riffing on strategy. We knew that world domination—or simply staying in business, in our case—would not happen without a lot of planning. We knew that Seattle and the Sub Pop bands, especially Nirvana, Tad, and Mudhoney, were generating interest globally. Our biggest challenge was keeping the organization afloat on limited resources. We were grateful to have a dedicated staff back in Seattle running things while we networked with European promoters and journalists.

After six hours of travel, we arrived just before dark in Paris's 10th Arrondissement. We hiked over to our hotel, dropped off our bags, and headed out for a walk to stretch our legs and talk some more. After a half an hour, we were getting cold and decided to head back. At that point, we realized we were lost. We had been so engrossed in conversation that we forgot to take note of the hotel address—or even the name of the place we were staying. As it got colder and darker, I thankfully discovered the hotel receipt in my pocket. A bit anxious, we headed back, ate dinner, and continued talking. There was a lot on our minds. In just two days, all three of our bands would join forces at the Astoria Theatre in London.

After we got back to the hotel, I called my fiancée, Hannah Parker, back in Seattle. Hannah had been doing a great job running our mail-order operation, which had been booming ever since we started our infamous Sub Pop Singles Club in October of 1988 with Nirvana's first record, "Love Buzz." Hannah had patiently and methodically hand-numbered all one thousand copies, which sold out and became collector's items.

Word from home was that the staff was doing well. The big news was that our friend and Seattle writer Nils Bernstein had managed to get Nirvana on the cover of Seattle magazine *The Rocket*. By remarkable coincidence, Nils had interviewed the band via phone on November 9, the historic day that the Berlin Wall fell.

They told Nils that while in Hannover, they had witnessed a flood of East Germans coming into the city to shop outside of Berlin for the first time since 1961. A few days later, Nirvana actually performed and rocked the newly liberated Berlin, unifying both East and West Germans, at Club Ecstasy. We were experiencing a revolutionary time.

Previous: Stopping over in Paris gave us time to reflect. I had studied French for three years in high school, not that I could speak it very well. Paris was our one day off, where Jon and I could relax a little bit and riff. Our working relationship then was really good. We had a natural tendency to brainstorm whenever we were together. I really appreciated that period of Sub Pop. We had financial constraints, but we could solve problems very quickly and move forward rapidly. Even though it looked like we were just traveling on a European vacation, we were basically talking about the label 24/7. We walked around Paris, talking, until we eventually got lost and had to concentrate on finding a train back to the hotel.

Overleaf: *The next morning we took the train to Caen where we caught a hovercraft ferry to Portsmouth, England, to meet up with the Mudhoney tour. Hovercraft service across the English Channel hasn't existed since about 2000. This ship looks dangerous, but seemed sleek and futuristic at the time. Coming from Seattle, the land of the Space Needle and the monorail, we felt right at home. I thought: "We're going to rock London, even if we have to ride on this crazy-ass boat!" The miracle that day was that everybody wound up in London. Everyone on the tour was broke by this point. We didn't have a lot of resources, so I'm impressed that we were able to get from point A to point B. In fact, Tad and Nirvana missed their ferry, so they did not arrive in London until forty minutes before their showcase, the biggest night yet of their careers. Somehow, we managed to pull it off.*

DAY 6
Portsmouth Polytechnic→ UK
Saturday, December 2

I was reluctant to leave the vibrancy of Paris behind so quickly. Ever since studying French as a student, I had envisioned visiting this city, with its historic appreciation for art and creativity. But in the early afternoon, after purchasing some pastries, we hopped aboard a train heading to the coastal city of Caen. From there, we sailed to Portsmouth, UK, to meet our good friends in Mudhoney, who were arriving from Manchester.

Jon and I arrived at the Portsmouth Polytechnic in time for soundcheck, and we were glad to see some familiar faces. Mudhoney was like family to us, they were the heart of the label at that time. Mudhoney's singer, Mark Arm, was a good friend, and he was an all-around scene maker back home. Guitarist Steve Turner was a remarkable punk scholar and record collector, always digging up rare tracks and turning me on to new bands. Drummer Dan Peters, bassist Matt Lukin, and manager Bob Whittaker all had the gift of being able to turn any moment into a party. I loved these guys.

At the time of our rendezvous, Mudhoney was in good spirits. They had a new record out, the self-titled *Mudhoney*, which was getting good reviews and climbing the UK Indie charts. They were Sub Pop's flagship band, and this was their third European tour. There was a huge buzz on the group, and they were the definitive headliners for the next day's LameFest UK showcase.

British indie icon Billy Childish, along with his band Thee Headcoats, was the opening act for the Portsmouth Polytechnic show. Steve Turner, Mudhoney's guitarist, had long been a champion of Childish, and this casual preshow soundcheck was the first time the two had met in person. The charming Mr. Childish, a former stonemason, was a self-taught painter and poet, as well as the most prolific indie recording artist I had ever met. At the time of this

Facing page: *Drummer Dan Peters and guitarist and vocalist Mark Arm of Mudhoney. To the best of my knowledge, Mark was the first person in Seattle to wear Mardi Gras beads.*

show, Childish, who typically fused poetic wordplay with primal garage punk, had self-released more than fifty albums; this in addition to publishing books of poetry and participating in gallery shows of his paintings. Mudhoney were notorious music geeks, visibly excited and honored to be doing the show with one of their idols.

After consuming some fish and chips and beer at a pub across the street, the bands were ready to entertain the students of Portsmouth Polytechnic. Thee Headcoats, traveling from Kent, succeeded in warming up the crowd with their direct, bluesy garage rock. "You Make Me Die," one of Billy's classics, and sounded brutish and loud.

A short break followed; then Mudhoney stepped onto the small stage to deliver their own brand of chaos.

Simply put, Mudhoney is one of the greatest live bands I've ever seen. At this show, they were at their peak, with catchy songs and an uncanny ability to fall apart and quickly reorganize. That night, the cheering audience was familiar with many of their songs, including "Touch Me I'm Sick" and "You Got It (Keep It Outta My Face)." Although the band's influences, like Blue Cheer, the Stooges, and the Sonics, were apparent, Mudhoney still managed to sound unique. They creatively used two vintage distortion pedals, the Superfuzz and the Big Muff, to add layers of texture to their songs. Infamously, their sets were never the same twice, as their performances were physical and spontaneous, brilliantly sloppy.

That night's show was ecstatic—as good as it gets. Everyone in the room was sweaty and blissed out. If this was any indication of what to expect at the London showcase, Seattle's imprint on the British music press would be huge. Grunge mania wasn't just hype; it was real.

Facing page: *I was very aware of Billy Childish, and I respected him a lot. We met in Portsmouth, and things really clicked. We decided we wanted to work together. I had an idea on the spot; I wanted Sub Pop to put out a double CD featuring one song from each of Billy's first fifty albums. The concept and execution came together in five minutes. He had never released anything on CD, and I thought the fact that someone had released fifty albums was creatively significant. When Sub Pop was really in the zone for me, I could have a crazy idea and see it become reality almost immediately. That was a very creative period for me.*

PortEnts PRESENTS

YARGO
PLUS SUPPORT

THURSDAY 12TH OCTOBER

ENTS HALL
**PORTSMOUTH POLY STUDENTS UNION
ALEXANDRA HOUSE. MUSEUM RD.
SOUTHSEA**

**DOORS 8PM · TICKETS £3·00 ADV
0705-819141   £3·50 DOOR**

NUS MEMBERS & GUESTS ONLY

PORTENTS PRESENTS

THE SOUP DRAGONS

**MONDAY 6th NOVEMBER
DOORS 8pm
PORTSMOUTH POLY STUDENT
MUSEUM ROAD SOUT
TICKETS £4/£4.50 PHONE**

PortEms

Z

POET

VEMBER

UTH POLY

S UNION

Tickets £3
819141

PortEms | S>U>B P<O<P

FROM ...ce U.S.A.

NIRVANA
AND
TAD
+ THE CATERAN

SATURDAY 28th OCTOBER
PORTSMOUTH POLY
STUDENTS UNION

Doors 8pm   Tickets £3.50

Further details 'phone (0705) 819141

NOT From cruddy ol' Portsmouth

Facing page: *Scenes from a British indie rock crowd circa 1989.* Above: *Dan Peters of Mudhoney surveys the scene.*

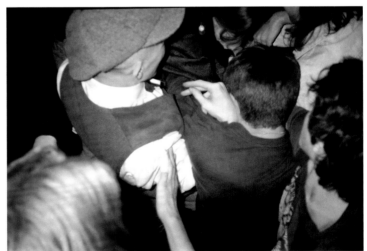

Facing page: *While Mark Arm deified Iggy Pop,
Mudhoney guitarist Steve Turner was a little more nerdy
and scholarly and thought Billy Childish was the man.
Steve was humbled in Billy's presence, and this was a
touching moment. These mutual admiration societies
within a network of hobbyists are what makes indie
music really fun—travelling and meeting people you
really respect. Mudhoney were such big fans of Billy*

*Childish that they covered his track "You Make Me Die."
Billy sang on the recording.* This page, bottom: *Rock
critic Everett True of* Melody Maker *was instrumental
in promoting Seattle grunge in the UK. Overleaf and
following: Opening attraction Billy Childish and Thee
Headcoats excite and delight fans and members of
Mudhoney.*

Above and following pages: *The crowd in Portsmouth was ecstatic—a common scene at Mudhoney shows as the band let it loose.*

Above and facing page: *Mudhoney regrouped backstage after another successful show. This was the calm before the storm.*

Astoria Theatre → London
Sunday, December 3

Nirvana, Tad, and Mudhoney. UK critics and fans had never experienced all three of these Seattle bands at one show before. We were excited, as we knew how powerful this combination was, having witnessed what took place at the Seattle LameFest. It was Sub Pop's dream to bring this posse to the UK, center of all knowing, and crush it. We expected validation, and we knew that if the bands delivered, the word would be amplified throughout the indie-rock universe. The US might even take notice.

Before the big show, Jon and I walked around London, enjoying the sights; then we took the tube train to the Astoria Theatre. Stopping by the venue, we noticed that the marquee only offered Mudhoney, with no mention of Nirvana or Tad, both of whom were newcomers to Europe. Soon, that would change.

As a large crowd started to gather outside, Tad and Nirvana finally arrived. They had missed a ferry coming over from France and were late for their soundchecks. The two bands flipped a coin to see who would open, and the luck of the draw determined that Nirvana would go first. Despite obstacles like temporary band breakups, stolen passports, and missed ferries, everyone was now gathered in London, which was very good news.

Jon and I tried to relax backstage with our support team, which included Reinhardt Holstein, the head of Sub Pop Europe, and Anton Brookes, our UK publicist. The theater was starting to fill up, on its way to being sold out. I drank beer with the musicians and then stepped out to look at the developing crowd. Some fans came dressed in flannel, which was very unusual in Britain. Others arrived already wearing Mudhoney or Nirvana T-shirts.

It was obvious that the audience had already built up their expectations. Earlier in the year, *Melody Maker* music critic Everett True had flown over to the U.S. and had personally confirmed that Seattle was indeed Sub Pop Rock City. BBC Radio 1 DJ John Peel had been playing our records, and had hyped us up in the London *Observer*. Now it was time to deliver.

The fans pushed forward as Nirvana walked onstage.

"Hello, we're one of the three official representatives of the Seattle Sub Pop scene from Washington State!" Kurt Cobain screeched into the microphone. Nirvana then tore into their typical opener, the riff-heavy "School." Rocking hard, Kurt immediately broke a string. Frustrated, he hustled off stage to replace it while Krist and Chad starting pounding out a Stooges cover, "I Wanna Be Your Dog." In the confusion, some of the crowd climbed onstage and began diving off.

"This is our last show of the tour, so we can do whatever the fuck we want!" yelled Krist.

Kurt rejoined the band, and Nirvana leaned into "Scoff," soon finding their momentum. Kurt's voice was soulful and intense. Kurt then leaped high and fell to his knees, beginning the guitar lines of their first single, "Love Buzz." The crowd went off and the tension mounted. Nirvana had energy and presence.

Seven more songs into the set, as they played their cover of "Molly's Lips," Kurt screamed out his enthusiasm for his favorite UK indie act. "This song was written by a band called the Vaselines! They're the best band in the world!"

More stage diving, this time from Matt Lukin and Mark Arm of Mudhoney, followed by Jon and me and others too numerous to mention. Tad finally threatened to jump, then backed off, relieving onlookers. The crowd was tranced-out and ecstatic. The show was going off.

That night, everything shifted. As the forty-five-minute set drew to a close, Nirvana finished with "Sappy," "Negative Creep," and "Blew." The band's grungy, primal punk-pop had won over the jaded London crowd, whose response was absolutely relentless. Mark Arm from Mudhoney looked on, speechless, at the band that was about to dethrone his own.

Kurt then pitched his guitar to Krist, who used his bass as a bat. Taking a big swing, Krist destroyed the recently purchased guitar. Thank God they were going home.

Tad and Mudhoney followed and put on heroic shows, winning over the crowd, but Nirvana was the epiphany of the evening. Clearly, LameFest UK marked the beginning of Nirvana's ascension. It was a turning point for Nirvana, for Sub Pop Records, and for rock history. Despite their status as an opening act, Nirvana had proven to London that they could fully captivate a large crowd. From here on, they would only get more popular.

Above: *We met up backstage with the musicians and our support team, including Reinhard Holstein, bottom left photo, the head of Sub Pop Europe, and Anton Brookes, lower right photo, our UK publicist. Partially pictured in topmost photo is the Sounds team of photographer Steve Double and journalist Keith Cameron.*

Above: *Shelli Dilley, Krist Novoselic, and Kurt Cobain. Shelli and Krist were married the following month.*

Above: *Sons of Washington State: Matt Lukin of Mudhoney and Kurt Cobain of Nirvana*

Above: *There was a great feeling of anticipation in the air—the smile on Tad Doyle's face at upper left says it all. We all knew what was about to hit London. In the lower right photo, Jon Poneman is wearing a LameFest UK shirt. That shirt was not our design at all. That was a very European take, and I'm not a really big fan of that shirt. That was a European take on rock and roll.*

Facing page: *LameFest UK sold out the 2,000-capacity Astoria Theatre. When Nirvana opened the show, many fans were still lined up in the lobby to buy T-shirts. We heard that members of happening British bands My Bloody Valentine, Senseless Things, The Faith Healers, and That Petrol Emotion were in the audience.*

Kurt Cobain screeched: "Hello, we're one of the three official representatives of the Seattle Sub Pop scene from Washington State!"—and the night was up and running. Nirvana, LameFest, 12/3/89

Within 15 seconds of Nirvana kicking into their set, Kurt broke
a string. Krist and Chad jammed on "I Wanna Be Your Dog" by
the Stooges while Kurt scrambled to restring his guitar.

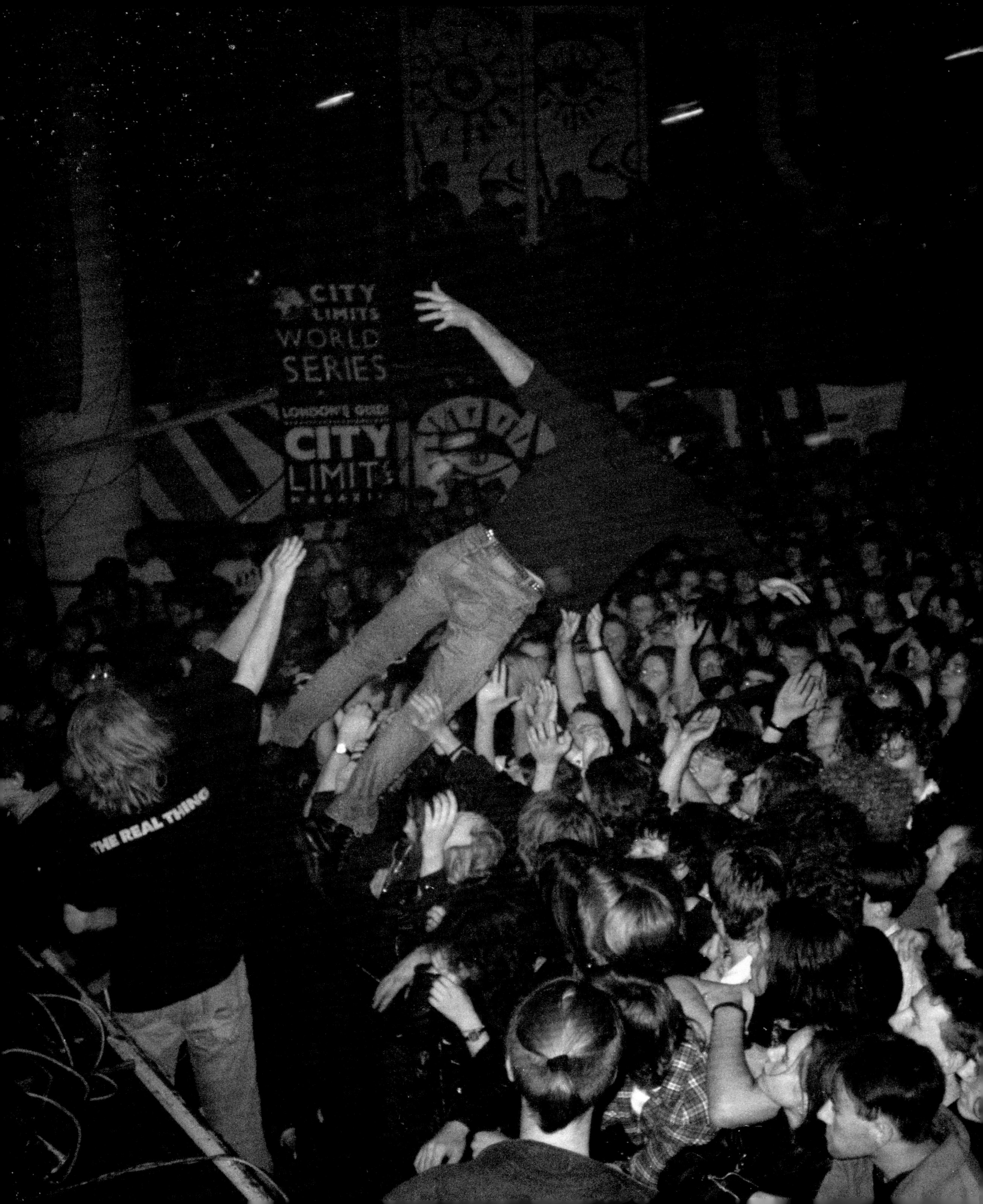
CITY LIMITS
WORLD SERIES
CITY LIMITS
THE REAL THING

Mudhoney's frontman Mark Arm couldn't believe the effect Nirvana was having on the crowd.

Above inset: *Mudhoney tour manager Erik Mans captured this gleeful photo of Kurt and Kris playing America's national pastime, using Kurt's new guitar as the baseball.* PHOTO BY ERIK MANS

THE REAL

In 1989, the stage presence of British bands was typically understated, while the stage presence of the Seattle bands was insanely overstated. When people saw the energy of our bands, they were totally blown away. Nobody stood still for a minute. The musicians were always in motion—jumping, falling on their knees, and leaping off amps. The bands were influenced by the Stooges, and they really took Iggy Pop's physicality to heart and brought that intensity to the stage. Iggy was a role model. The performances by all three bands were awesome, as usual. What was typical for us was a revelation to the UK crowd.

Toiling at the Coalface of Pop Culture

Steve Double

I worked for *Sounds*. I was freelance, and the magazine would regularly send me to parts of the world to cover gigs or photograph bands that did not particularly want to be photographed. I loved music and I loved photography, and I indulged in both of them and got paid.

At least, I loved *most* of the bands that *Sounds* covered. Within a month of photographing the bands at LameFest UK, I also photographed Skid Row, Grant Hart of Hüsker Dü, Rollins Band, the Stone Roses at Alexandra Palace, the Sugarcubes, and Bon Jovi. You can try to guess who rated as top of my pops and who didn't.

I never saw a contract, and *Sounds* and I never had a gentleman's agreement. Our arrangement was more like honor among thieves. I myself paid for the film, processing, and printing. The magazine awarded me a reproduction fee based on the size of the image they ran. Consequently, each roll of film was precious. If I shot loads of film and the mag only ran a small shot, I could actually lose money. The basic economics were very much in mind that same month just mentioned, as I also photographed Furniture, Last Few Days, Kev Hopper, Dan Reed, Skint Video, and Sensible Footwear. I had to artfully gauge how big the piece would be and which images they would use.

For a gig like the Sub Pop showcase, usually I would just shoot the headliners. *Sounds* never needed pictures of the support acts—and even down the road, who would ever need three rolls of film of Sensible Footwear? But the mag was big into Sub Pop, so I knew in advance that I would be shooting for a full-page special. As far as I knew, Mudhoney was the name band poised to break first. John Peel played them all the time. They had been to the UK before, and I had already photographed them. Nirvana? Well, I'd heard of them, but their music hadn't grabbed me immediately. *Sounds* scribe Keith Cameron saw the magic in *Bleach*, though. Since the magazine trusted Keith's writing, the live editor told me to shoot all three bands that Sunday night.

More than twenty years later, I remember almost embarrassingly unimportant details that in themselves tell the story about what mattered. The evening was cold. I wore only a T-shirt. I had to be at the venue before the doors opened, as Nirvana would be playing onstage ten minutes after the crowd was allowed inside. The doors opened late, though, so I froze my tits off. I remember having a little complain to Anton, Sub Pop's press agent.

I don't remember the stage divers pictured. I don't remember a note of Nirvana's performance. Through looking at my images, I recall that Kurt lobbed his guitar at Chris's bass, like a pitcher with a baseball—but I don't have a real memory of that happening. To be sure, LameFest UK was just another gig for me. Nirvana was not a band I might have particularly expected to hear again. Given the weight of evidence, they would more likely become a Barracudas than a Bon Jovi.

Yet picking over the photographic vestiges of Kurt's life again brings me back to my past life as a toiler at the coalface of popular culture. The images draw out strange swirls of emotion, shaded by the fatal pitfalls of fame. I see this performer's need to create and express and act out, balanced dangerously against a need for vindication and the fight against becoming another cog in the machine. And I'm faced with my part in all of this. At the end of the day, as I think these photos display clearly, it's only rock 'n' roll—but we have good cause to love it.

Previous page: *This is a photo by Steve Double of me, Bruce Pavitt, onstage behind Nirvana at LameFest UK. I have my trusty pocket camera in hand. In a few pages it looks like I'm about to take a photo, but no such picture exists. So where's my picture of this epic bass-smashing moment? I must have finally ran out of film, sadly. Fortunately, Steve Double was there taking some of the best Nirvana live shots I've ever seen.* PREVIOUS PAGE, FACING PAGE, AND ALL FOLLOWING B&W PHOTOGRAPHS BY STEVE DOUBLE

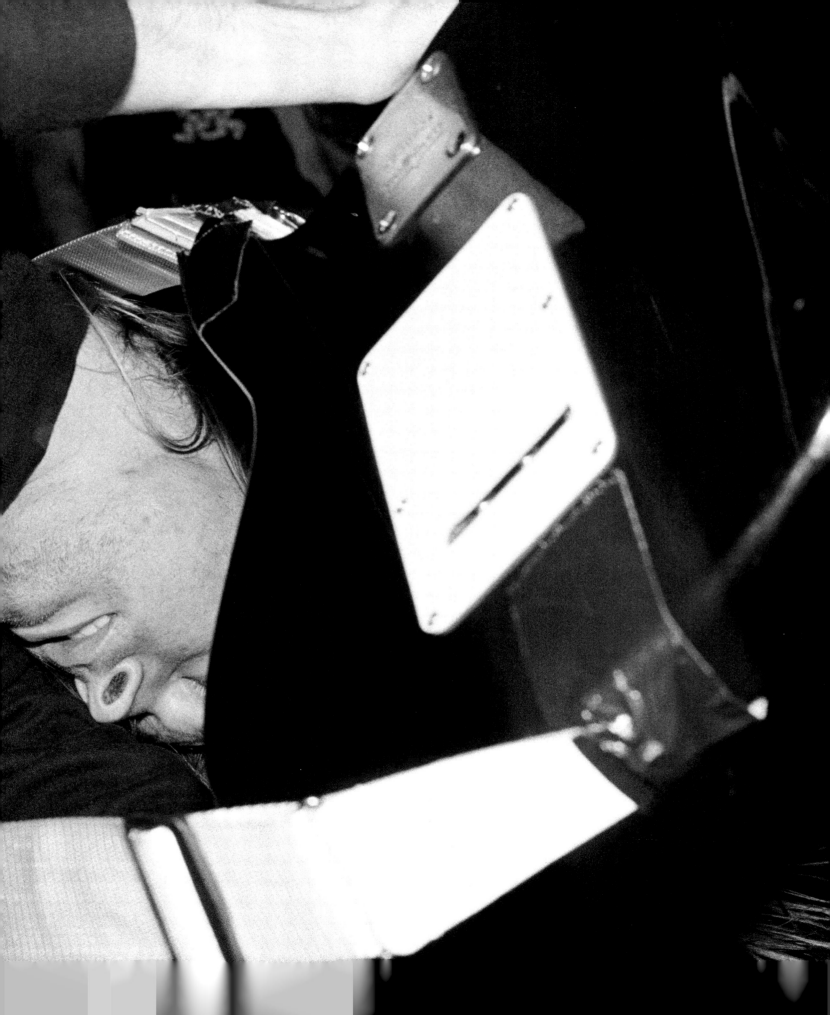

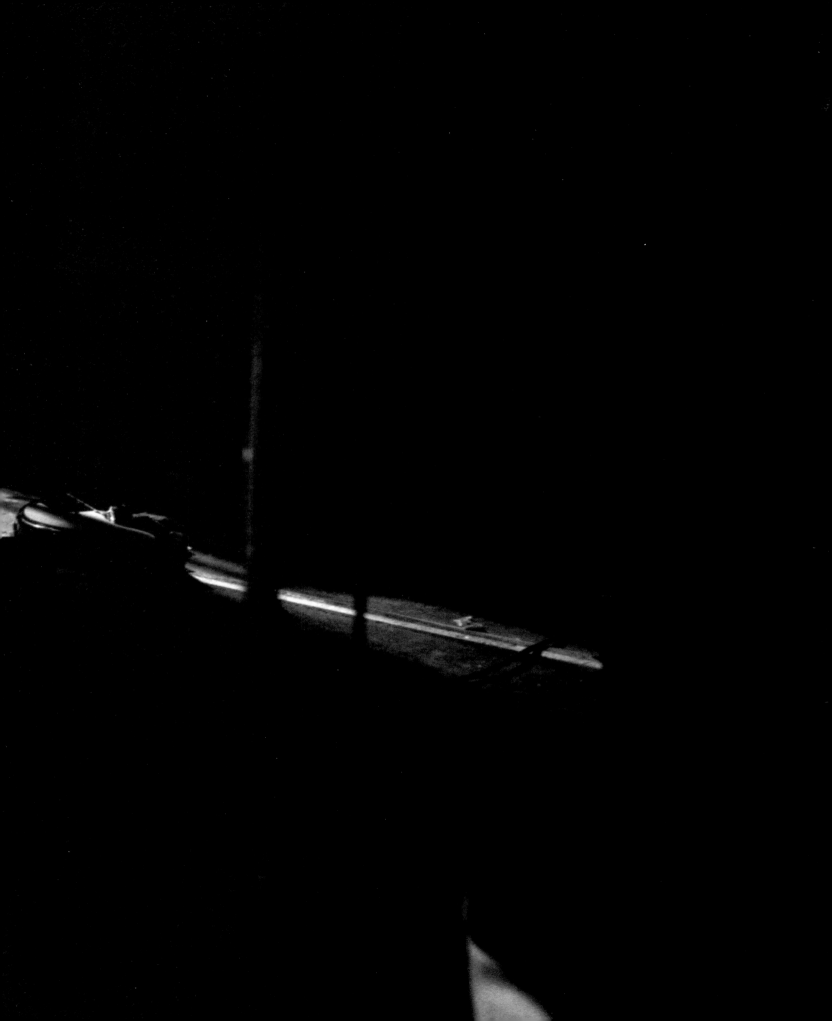

Kurt talked enthusiastically with this fan and me about the Vaselines. Within two years Nirvana would be a global sensation. We were thankful that they eventually released a cover of "Molly's Lips" by the Vaselines for the Sub Pop Singles Club. At this point, having a Sub Pop bin (see far left) here seemed pretty cool.

This page, from top: *Tad always knew how to make an entrance; Big props to Reinhard Holstein, of Glitterhouse Recs. and Sub Pop Europe. Sub Pop would not be in business today if not for him. I was dating a girl from Denver who told me about a Denver group called the Fluid, that fit in with what we were doing. They were on Glitterhouse Recs. from Germany, so I reached out and made an agreement to put out the Fluid records in the U.S.. Reinhard visited Jon and I, and we started offering slightly different pressings with collectors in mind. We would release them in Europe, and then Australia, and those would be a little different. Reinhard occasionally sent us cash when we needed it, and he made sure our records were in stores in Europe. He also pressed 12" singles, which indie bands in the States just didn't do. That was a very boutique thing, but I think it gave Mudhoney and the others a little more prestige. We were blessed to have had a working relationship with him. Facing page, from top: Mark Arm of Mudhoney at Rough Trade; Excited fan holding the Nirvana "Blew" 12", which went to number one on the UK Indie chart the following month. Overleaf: Mudhoney, Astoria Theatre, London, 12/4/89, view from cloud nine.*

Aftermath

The British Music Press

Traveling around Europe in 1989, we and the Sub Pop bands had more than our passports validated. During the pre-Internet 1980s, it was difficult for struggling regional bands in the United States to achieve any national media attention. In England, the situation was different. Competing UK music weeklies like *Sounds*, *Melody Maker,* and *NME*—the *New Musical Express*—provided media opportunities for any bands willing to tour there.

The following interviews and live reviews give you a sense of the impact Nirvana, Tad, and Mudhoney made on the British press during the fall of 1989. The covers of these periodicals portray what was dominating the music media at this particular moment—Happy Mondays, Stone Roses, and Guns 'N Roses—and the layouts capture a sense of how things looked at the time. This was also the dawn of desktop publishing, that much is clear.

An initial buzz based on our records generated real enthusiasm, and that hype and excitement became respect after the bands delivered the raw goods live. Nirvana, Tad, Mudhoney, and Sub Pop pulled off a minor miracle, and the moment of impact deserves a little bit of further analysis. We the representatives of Washington went abroad hoping for the best, and at the end of the journey I would say we made our mark.

"By the time they tour Europe with Tad this coming October, Nirvana's future as the next *big* thing will be in the bag...Tad plan to travel over with Nirvana (in the same bus!) for their European tour...Let's just hope there's a hall big enough to hold their enormous sound."—tour preview by Edwin Pouncey, *NME*, September 2, 1989

"Feel the Noise. Everywhere you go, everywhere you look, Britain is being swamped in a deluge of long hair, hoary old Black Sabbath licks, and American upstarts from Seattle. Where

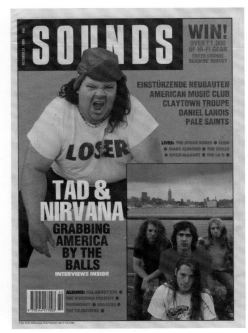

Above: *I had followed the British music papers since even before launching my* Sub Pop *fanzine in 1980. The lack of coverage of American indie bands was always maddening. So to see Tad and Nirvana on the cover of* Sounds *was very gratifying.* Sounds *even beat Seattle's hometown music paper* The Rocket *to the punch!*

Nirvana differs from most of their contemporaries is in the strength of [Kurt Cobain's] song-writing. Kurdt Kobain is the vocalist, guitarist, and main songwriter behind [Nirvana]. He's your archetypal small guy—wiry, defiantly working class, and fiery. His provincial and witty lyrics bring to mind an American Mark E. Smith. He has a small goatee and his pet rat once bit Bruce Pavitt, Sub Pop records supremo."—Everett True, *Melody Maker*, October 21, 1989

"Scrawny bar-chord operatives, Nirvana are the small town kids let loose in the middle-aged music biz grind. Their onstage, guerrilla insurrections and scuzzed pop punk anthems are just about heroic enough to push through the Nirvana-as-Sub-Pop's-trump card prediction made by some old fool a couple months back."—John Robb, *Sounds*, October 21, 1989

"If we hadn't done this band thing, we would have been doing what everyone else does back home, which is chopping down trees , drinking, having sex and drinking, talking about sex, and drinking some more."—Kurt Cobain, *Sounds*, October 21, 1989

"Of all the Sub Pop bands, Tad looks to have the greatest longevity—something that stems from their unprecedented welding of the comic to the cauterizing. Thriving on the ability to top the parody of tree-felling macho bigotry that makes up their interviews ("Music's just a good way to unwind after a hard day wood-choppin' and masturbatin'."), onstage Tad also displays a serious musical alter ego...Fielding Nirvana after Tad was a tactical error tonight. Having lost guitarist Jason Everman to Soundgarden, Nirvana were a shadow of the teen thug combo that played the New York Music Seminar earlier this year."—live review by Roy Wilkinson, *Sounds*, November 4, 1989

"Tad the band makes music that is bulky and unstoppable, gorged on elephantine riffs and vast drum stampedes. Songs are thrown up with gonzoid glee, and the crowd devours them like a pack of hyenas would a hunk of fresh meat. The man himself bangs and heaves like Meat Loaf's psychotic nephew, hands like sides of beef wringing hell out of his guitar, the most perfect antithesis of America's endless supply of glammed-up chicks-with-dicks to ever stomp a stage."—live review by Neil Perry, *Melody Maker*, November 4, 1989

"Kurdt Cobain has a voice to reduce grown men to tears, and the sort of hoarse, anguished cry that can turn a good song into an unforgettable one. Nirvana work from their own rock blueprint, pushing their songs through an emotional and physical grinder, each one edging towards a private precipice inside Kobain's mind...You can't argue or reason with stuff like this. Nirvana were superb, cranked-up, desperate and f***ing loud."—live review by Neil Perry, *Melody Maker*, November 4, 1989

"Doubtless we are influenced by the past and dig a lot of music back then, just like we dig Mudhoney, Nirvana, and the Fluid, but whether through incompetence or design, we try to twist things up more, distort our influences and spit them out in a mangled fashion...in such a way that you won't recognize it."—Kurt Danielson, Tad, *Melody Maker*, November 11, 1989

"All hyped-up with nowhere to go, except the next town at the end of the next freeway, Mud-honey are ultimate rock escapism—a catharsis as much for their benefit as the crowd's... Mudhoney successfully manoeuvre the thin line that separates inspiration and contrivance. This must go some way to explain their success in Britain, where rock audiences are weaned largely on self-conscious, stylized imitations...Whether or not they are, Mudhoney appear The Real Thing. They convince."—Keith Cameron, *Sounds*, November 18, 1989

"We're not on a major label, so we can do whatever we want."—Mark Arm, *Sounds*, November 18,1989

"Have we embraced Mudhoney purely for their transatlantic trendiness? Is the Seattle/Sub Pop sound ringing only in the ears of scoop-searching parasites? No, no, and hell no. Just ask the people who regularly occupy the stage at Mudhoney gigs as if it was sacred ground... Barely seconds into Mudhoney's virulent opener, Mark leaps from the tiny stage into the crowd, who are so tightly packed that he literally walks at least ten foot deep into the throng... Somewhere in the venue an alarm bell goes off. It is ignored."—live review by Neil Perry, *Melody Maker*, December 2, 1989

"Mudhoney at the Riverside ... well it was everything we could have looked for, really. Sweat, stamina, steam, sinews, stage-diving, sex, spontaneity, swan-diving, singles, and serendipity. Oh, and raw vulnerability. During the finale...Steve attempted a headstand on his guitar, Mark was torn limb-from-limb after leaping into the baying crowd, Matt toppled over backwards, and Dan staged a one-handed drum solo. Afterwards the band sat around arguing about how to top that as the kids screamed, ever more frantic, for an encore."—live review by Everett True, *Melody Maker*, December 2, 1989

Facing page: *The UK press wielded a lot of clout. The approval of* Sounds, NME, *and* Melody Maker *played a big role in pushing things forward for Nirvana, Tad, and Mudhoney back in the States.*

LIVE!

FLAT OUT F**ED

MUDHONEY
RIVERSIDE, NEWCASTLE

F***, YEAH! "I'm crawling out of my skin/I wanna get into you again!" What a great name (waddagreatname-waddagreatname!) Mudhoney. Images spring to mind, almost unbidden; of hippos wallowing and ladies wrestling, of bees and birds and sickly sweet lemon drinks oozing off spoons, of grunge and grease, dirt tempered with delight, shit and treacle. F*** YEAH! "Where are you going tonight, petal?" "Just out to wallow in some mud, honey."

Mudhoney at the Riverside . . . well it was everything we could have looked for; really. Sweat, stamina, steam, sinews, stage-diving, sex, spontaneity, swan-diving, singles and serendipity. Oh, and *raw* vulnerability. It was during the finale, "In-N-Out Of Grace," I believe, that Steve attempted a headstand on his guitar, Mark was torn limb-from-limb after leaping into the baying crowd, Matt toppled over backwards and Dan staged a one-handed drum solo. Afterwards the band sat around arguing about how to top *that* as the kids screamed, ever more frantic, for an encore. "But we're an honest band," Mark argued. "We're just not into wanton acts of destruction." Too right son. As the song put it, "Flat Out F***ed." Tonight the Mudhoney roadshow come to town and there wasn't a dry armpit in the house.

"Magnolia Caboose Babyshit" opens proceedings — a lamebrain instrumental in the grand tradition of Hendrix played badly with the amps up full — oh, hi, Blue Cheer, didn't see you waiting in the wings there. "Get Into Yours" is a megalithic metallic crunch, a slamdriver, four boys confronting the seamy side of love and revelling in it, an acid trip with the auto-pilot set on reverse.

Mudhoney aren't simple '69 (or '71, '73, '76, '79, '83 or whatever damn year it is out there) revivalists,

however. Their music — call it metal, call it rock 'n' roll, call it blues, just don't call it dumb — is far too up-and-in-your-face for that. All Mudhoney do, like any other band worth their salt, is to listen to their influences, take what they need, and then decimate them. Make them seem ridiculous and beside the point. So you can hear bits of the Sabs, Minor Threat, Hendrix, and The Stooges, say, in "Come To Mind," "Dead Love" and "Touch Me I'm Sick", say? What the f***?! Get the hell out of our way. We've some serious self-mutilation to do here!

So "If I Think" is the most frenetic, cranium-crunching, torso-twisting, libido-enlivening song we hear until, oh, the C&W tinted (I kid you not) "Running Loaded," which *kicks ass into orbit.* So they don't play "Here Comes Sickness," chucking their references to "dogs sniffing

round your crotch" into several other unsavoury numbers instead. So "Mud Ride" is near unrecognisable (as any encore rightly should be), steeped in vibrato and a grisly beat. So? Come closer. Enjoy the ride. Shit, this coaster ain't gonna last much longer at this pace.

Mudhoney finish with "Hate The Police." We were incapable of even thinking.

EVERETT TRUE

PICS: STEPHEN SWEET

SOUNDS

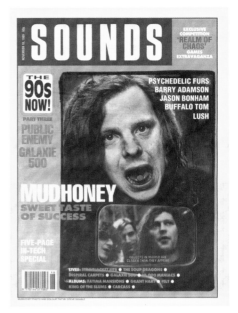

EXCLUSIVE COMPETITION 'REALM OF CHAOS' GAMES EXTRAVAGANZA

THE 90s NOW!

PSYCHEDELIC FURS
BARRY ADAMSON
JASON BONHAM
BUFFALO TOM
LUSH

PART THREE
PUBLIC ENEMY
GALAXIE 500

MUDHONEY
SWEET TASTE OF SUCCESS

FIVE-PAGE HI-TECH SPECIAL

TAD
NIRVANA
LONDON ASTORIA

SLIM PICKIN'S?!

Confessions of a Ticket Tout

JON BON JOVI "I am the fifth most famous man in Rock"

NME

SUDDEN DEF
KILT
The hairy horror of The Kilt in Rock

(Meet the first)

JIMMY SOMERVILLE
SIR NODDY HOLDER
INSPIRAL CARPETS
GREEN ON RED
KEITH LEVENE
SONIC BOOM
ERASURE
FUGAZI

U2 IN JAPAN Exclusive!

MELODY·MAKER

OCTOBER 21 1989 WEEKLY 50p

KATE BUSH
SENSUAL HEALING

ALBUMS
TERENCE TRENT D'ARCY
ERASURE
DEBORAH HARRY
THE BEAUTIFUL SOUTH
WEDDING PRESENT
COSTELLO

MELODY MAKER, October 21 1989 47

NIRVANA
BLEACHED WAILS

EVERETT TRUE THRASHES IT OUT WITH THE LATEST WIZARDS FROM SEATTLE'S SUB POP LABEL WHO ARRIVE IN BRITAIN NEXT WEEK. PICS: ANDY CATLIN

"Contrary to popular belief, we are not superstars and that's why we're playing so much. If it was a big pressure we wouldn't do it. . ."
– Dan Peters

BIG CHIEF

mud,
sweat
and
beers

Mudhoney – the coolest, the smartest, the sexiest of the Sub Pop mob – are punching holes in the ozone layer and running out of Bud with their explosive world tour. Keith Cameron joins them in the States and tries their punishing schedule. Steve Double gets in training

---

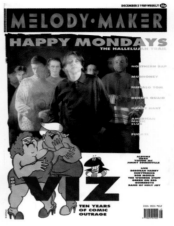

Above: *Thurston Moore of Sonic Youth, Gibby Haynes of Butthole Surfers, and J. Mascis of Dinosaur Jr. appearing on the cover of* Melody Maker *was another sign of the times.*

Melvins) at Reciprocal Studios, not realizing it was *the* place to record. Producer Jack Endino turned a copy of the tape over to Jonathan Poneman at Sub Pop, who immediately contacted the band to negotiate a deal for a single.

The resultant single was released in early 1988 and included a devastating (through sitar-less) covering of Shocking Blue's "Love Buzz" as well as a great, anthemic original called "Big Cheese." Despite no headlining shows in Seattle and virtually no local media coverage, the single's limited edition of 1000 sold out as fast as any Sub Pop release up to that point. Today the single is quite collectible, valued at around $30.

Nirvana, now with third (and final) drummer Chad Channing, by this time had solidified into a certifiable "power trio." Throughout 1988 the band increased their growing following with a number of deadly live shows, featuring Channing's manic blur, Novoselic's menacing six-foot-plus presence, and the hearty wails of Kobain, whose passionate vocal style, in the words of one *Melody Maker* writer, "has been known to reduce grown men and women to tears."

The long-awaited *Bleach* album was recorded for an unheard-of $600 and released in early 1989. Considered by some critics to be one of only a handful of Sub Pop releases of any lasting value, *Bleach* (the first 1000 of which were issued on white vinyl and now fetch up to $25) was hailed by most and worshipped by many. As noisy as any Sub Pop record, *Bleach* also contains a strong sense of melody and careful song construction which have done much to dispel much of the cynicism surrounding the Sub Pop label.

A second guitarist, Jason Everman, was added after the recording of the album but before its release. His appearance on both the sleeve and credits of *Bleach* led people to believe that he played on the album. In fact, he was added solely for touring purposes and put on the album simply to integrate him more fully into the band. His split over "artistic differences" was "a very mutual decision," says Kobain. "He just wasn't into exactly the right type of music, especially for the direction that we're going now." (Everman has since gone on to replace Hiro Yamamoto as bass player for Soundgarden.)

As for the band's new direction, Kobain says, "We're writing a lot more pop songs, like 'About a Girl'...some people might think of that as 'changing' into something, but it's something we've always been aware of and are just now starting to express. The stuff we're listening to now are I guess what are called 'cutie bands' in England—Beat Happening, Pixies, Shonen Knife, Young Marble Giants—right now my favorite band is the Vaselines.

"My biggest influence was punk rock for sure," he continues. "I was weaned on hard rock like Led Zeppelin, Skin Diver, Aerosmith, and especially the Beatles when I was younger. I'd been kind of developing this style of intense, hard, 'grungy,' punk-rock-meets-hard-rock for a couple years before we started this band, and then it really developed when we got together and started writing the songs."

A limited edition, 4-song 12-inch EP was recently issued in England on the Tupelo label (which also issued *Bleach* overseas, substituting "Big Cheese" for "Love Buzz"). Featuring "Blew" and "Love Buzz" from the album, it also includes two new songs, recorded With Steve Fisk. "Stain" and "Been a Son" hint at the direction Nirvana is heading with their next record, slated for release next spring.

Coming from Aberdeen and all, Nirvana have too often —especially in the British press—fallen victim to overeager critics romanticizing their "humble origins" and their "triumph" over them. Stuff like, "hailing from the redneck backwoods of Aberdeen, Washington, Nirvana unleash a desperate wail born of a lifetime of small-town frustration," etc., etc. While Kobain concedes that there's a little truth in that somewhere, it's an impression they're working hard to overcome.

"I feel like we've been tagged as illiterate redneck cousin-fucking kids that have no idea what's going on at all. That's completely untrue."

NIRVANA

BERLIN IS JUST A STATE OF MIND

by Nils Bernstein

"It's kinda gross, really." Chris Novoselic, bassist for Nirvana, is describing The Invasion Of The Brainwashed/Stonewashed East Germans from a hotel in Hamburg. In Europe supporting their debut LP on Sub Pop, *Bleach*, Nirvana arrived in Berlin with co-headliners Tad in the midst of what appeared to be the beginnings of national unification. "All these little cars."

But has Nirvana witnessed history-in-the-making?

"We didn't even know what was going on until a little before we got to the border and there were all these little cars crammed full of people offering us fruit," Novoselic continues. "I heard one man cried at the sight of bananas," adds singer Kurdt Kobain.

Detractors will say what they will about Sub Pop and, by association, Nirvana, but they've got to be doing something right. On the strength of one acid-warped, ooops-there-went-a-pop-song, hard rock masterpiece of an album (plus a little help from the Sub Pop hype machine), they've landed themselves in Europe, packing 1000-capacity venues, with an album in the UK Indie Top Ten, and their name mentioned so regularly in the British music press that at this point we're simply supposed to *know* who they're talking about.

Nirvana came together a few years ago in classic garage-band fashion, when Kobain and Novoselic, living in Aberdeen, made a demo tape with Dale (drummer for the Melvins) at Reciprocal Studios, not realizing it was *the* place to record. Producer Jack Endino turned a copy of the tape over to Jonathan Poneman at Sub Pop, who immediately contacted the band to negotiate a deal for a single.

The resultant single was released in early 1988 and included a devastating (though sitar-less) cover of Shocking Blue's "Love Buzz" as well as a great, anthemic original called "Big Cheese." Despite no headlining shows in Seattle and virtually no local media coverage, the single's limited edition of 1000 sold out as fast as any Sub Pop release up to that point. Today the single is quite collectible, valued at around $30.

Nirvana, now with third (and final) drummer Chad Channing, by this time had solidified into a certifiable "power trio." Throughout 1988 the band increased their growing following with a number of deadly live shows, featuring Channing's manic blur, Novoselic's menacing six-foot-plus presence, and the hearty wails of Kobain, whose passionate vocal style, in the words of one *Melody Maker* writer, "has been known to reduce grown men and women to tears."

The long-awaited *Bleach* album was recorded for an unheard-of $600 and released in early 1989. Considered by some critics to be one of only a handful of Sub Pop releases of any lasting value, *Bleach* (the first 1000 of which were issued on white vinyl and now fetch up to $25) was hailed by most and worshipped by many. As noisy as any Sub Pop record, *Bleach* also contains a strong sense of melody and careful song construction which have done much to dispel much of the cynicism surrounding the Sub Pop label.

A second guitarist, Jason Everman, was added after the recording of the album but before its release. His appearance on both the sleeve and credits of *Bleach* led people to believe that he played on the album. In fact, he was added solely for touring purposes and put on the album simply to integrate him more fully into the band. His split over "artistic differences" was "a very mutual decision," says Kobain. "He just wasn't into exactly the right type of music, especially for the direction that we're going now." (Everman has since gone on to replace Hiro Yamamoto as bass player for Soundgarden.)

As for the band's new direction, Kobain says, "We're writing a lot more pop songs, like 'About a Girl'... some people might think of that as 'changing' into something, but it's something we've always been aware of and are just now starting to express. The stuff we're listening to now are I guess what are called 'cutie bands' in England — Beat Happening, Pixies, Shonen Knife, Young Marble Giants — right now my favorite band is the Vaselines.

"My biggest influence was punk rock for sure," he continues. "I was weaned on hard rock like Led Zeppelin, Skin Diver, Aerosmith, and especially the Beatles when I was younger. I'd been kind of developing this style of intense, hard, 'grungy,' punk-rock-meets-hard-rock for a couple years before we started this band, and then it really developed when we got together and started writing the songs."

A limited edition, 4-song 12-inch EP was recently issued in England on the Tupelo label (which also issued *Bleach* overseas, substituting "Big Cheese" for "Love Buzz"). Featuring "Blew" and "Love Buzz" from the album, it also includes two new songs, recorded with Steve Fisk. "Stain" and "Been a Son" hint at the direction Nirvana is heading with their next record, slated for release next spring.

Coming from Aberdeen and all, Nirvana have too often — especially in the British press — fallen victim to overeager critics romanticizing their "humble origins" and their "triumph" over them. Stuff like, "hailing from the redneck backwoods of Aberdeen, Washington, Nirvana unleash a desperate wail born of a lifetime of small-town frustration," etc., etc. While Kobain concedes that there's a little truth in that somewhere, it's an impression they're working hard to overcome.

"I feel like we've been tagged as illiterate redneck cousin-fucking kids that have no idea what's going on at all. That's completely untrue."

"I feel like we've been tagged as illiterate redneck cousin-fucking kids that have no idea what's going on at all. That's completely untrue."

Front ends overleaf: *Kurt Cobain of Nirvana, LameFest UK, Astoria Theatre, London, 12/3/89*. STEVE DOUBLE.
Front ends, next page: *Cobain walking under the palm trees of Rome, 11/28/89*. BRUCE PAVITT. This page: *Krist Novoselic, Nirvana, LameFest UK*. BRUCE PAVITT. Next overleaf: *Mark Arm of Mudhoney, LameFest UK*. STEVE DOUBLE